Practical INDOOR GARDENING

Yvonne Rees

The Crowood Press

First published in 1994 by
The Crowood Press Ltd
Ramsbury, Marlborough
Wiltshire SN8 2HR

© The Crowood Press Ltd 1994

All rights reserved. No part of this publication may be reproduced or transmitted in any form or by any means, electronic or mechanical, including photocopy, recording, or any information storage and retrieval system, without permission in writing from the publishers.

British Library Cataloguing-in-Publication Data

A catalogue record for this book is available from the British Library.

ISBN 1 85223 779 1

Acknowledgements

Picture Credits
All photographs by Ian Murray except those on page 1 which is reproduced by courtesy of Sandersons, pages 2/3 which is reproduced by courtesy of Dobies Seeds and those on pages 20 (right) and 61, which are by Yvonne Rees.
Line-drawings by Claire Upsdale-Jones.

Typeset in Optima by Chippendale Type Ltd,
Otley, West Yorkshire
Printed and bound by Paramount Printing Group, Hong Kong

CONTENTS

	INTRODUCTION	4
1	CHOOSING HOUSEPLANTS	5
2	PROPAGATION	9
3	PLANTS AROUND THE HOME	16
4	EXOTIC PLANTS	25
5	POTS, TERRARIA AND BOTTLES	32
6	CARE AND MAINTENANCE	46
7	SOMETHING FOR ALL SEASONS	56
	GLOSSARY	62
	INDEX	64

INTRODUCTION

No room looks complete without at least one leafy plant as living decoration. From the humblest home to the office reception or hotel foyer, foliage and flowering plants are considered to be as essential as all the other carefully chosen furnishings and accessories. They certainly help soften the harder lines of furniture and interior architecture: trailing and climbing houseplants frequently hang in growing curtains from shelves and brackets. Dramatic large-leaved specimens like the Swiss cheese plant (*Monstera deliciosa*) can be used to add interest to a dull corner, especially at night when the giant foliage can be cleverly spotlighted from below to throw exaggerated shadows; or it can act as a partial screen positioned in front of the window.

Shorter-lived flowering plants can be colour co-ordinated to your interior scheme; varieties are even being bred to match current colour trends and are invaluable for adding a splash of living colour to the dining table, plant-stand or windowsill. Plants should be a regular item on your shopping list and their care part of your daily routine, for they are undoubtedly the making of a successful and enjoyable interior. But this is true only for as long as they are healthy, happy and looking good; nothing looks worse than a sad and sorry specimen, with leaves that are drooping or discoloured.

The most important step towards successful and good-looking houseplants is to choose the right plant. Most plants have quite specific needs when it comes to light, warmth and water requirements. Your home will usually offer a great many independent mini-environments, so it should be possible to accommodate a number of different plant types. One factor that must be taken into account is whether a room is heated or not. Light levels are particularly important as these control how and when a plant usually flowers: for example, poinsettias are 'short-day' plants, producing blooms as the days shorten; fuchsias are 'long day' plants, requiring longer days in order to produce their distinctive dangling flowers. Humidity, too, will vary from room to room and those plants which prefer a humid, even steamy, atmosphere will do best in the kitchen or bathroom, not the arid environment of the centrally heated living-room. Like watering and feeding, these conditions can be artificially controlled but only to a limited degree.

Selecting the right plant for the position available within the home is half the battle, but giving each the right care is equally important. Watering is by far the biggest cause of problems, with as many plants dying from over-zealous watering as from lack of it. You must learn the requirements of all your houseplants and give each what it needs as and when it needs it, not a general soaking for one and all when you remember or find the time. Plants, especially flowering species, will need feeding during the growing season as pots can offer only limited resources. In winter some plants need to be 'rested' without food, water or even much light for several months; others might require a 'top-up' light source such as a grow-bulb to extend their day during the summer.

Knowing a little about your plants will not only help you to look after them correctly, but will give you a great deal of pleasure, too, as you come to know each more closely. As their needs and moods become familiar to you, you will begin to understand the philosophy of 'talking to your houseplants to keep them happy'; it is that day-to-day contact that keeps them healthy. That said, there are some plants – usually the flowering species – which are intended to be only short-lived and which after several months of a fine display are meant to be discarded and replaced. The following chapters will help you to become better acquainted with the needs of the different types of houseplant, and thus to achieve the best results.

1 • CHOOSING HOUSEPLANTS

It may happen that you are completely seduced by a certain specimen at your local petrol garage or supermarket, and so delighted by its attractive or unusual appearance (or its low price) that you buy the plant on impulse, relying on its plastic label or maybe a book such as this one to give some guidance on where to put it and how to look after it when you get home. Often, plants are given as presents and, again, the recipient will have to decide in retrospect whether there is a suitable place to put it

Free-flowering plants like these beautiful elatior begonias and regal pelargoniums really bring the brightness and freshness of summer into the home, but they must be in peak condition to continue blooming as well as this.

***Aucuba japonica* 'Variegata'** The spotted laurel has bright green glossy leaves splashed with yellow and is a useful hardy plant to brighten gloomy corners as it will tolerate partial shade to shade. This plant prefers cool conditions; minimum temperature 4.5°C (40°F). The leaves tend to fall off in a hot, dry atmosphere. Given a cool shady spot, the *Aucuba* grows well and is likely to need an occasional prune to prevent it getting out of hand.

and make an informed guess at how to look after it. Unfortunately plant labels are frequently unreliable or just plain useless, being so general that they tell you virtually nothing at all: 'foliage plant; moderate warmth and light' is a popular one. It is far more satisfying, where you can, to explore the possibilities outlined in Chapter 3 (which covers the types of plant you can choose for specific positions within your home), and then to go out and buy those specimens wherever possible from a reputable stockist.

There are several drawbacks to the impulse buy. Firstly, the kind of outlet where you will see such plants on offer is not really geared to the care of plants but to encouraging you to spend a little extra money when you are really buying something else. Thus they will seek to catch your attention with a crowded, brightly lit display, extremely low prices or fancy packaging,

6 · Practical Indoor Gardening

You often see potted plants like this striking Aster 'Pinocchio' *on sale in supermarkets and outside petrol stations, but the plants are likely to be grimed or will have shrivelled buds due to pollution or poor care.*

what is often a subtropical or similar tender species; they have neither the natural light, the correct levels of warmth and coolness, nor the humidity required to keep plants in good condition. The plants' care will be cursory and usually unskilled, which reduces even further their chances of survival once you get them home. A few supermarkets are trying to rectify this by giving their staff a little training in plant care and by issuing each plant with a sell-by date, but you still cannot beat the custom-made environment of a horticultural specialist where trained personnel are on hand to answer your queries.

The other problem with buying plants on impulse is that you will probably not be prepared for transporting them home: it is virtually impossible to get plants home unscathed when they are improperly wrapped or packaged, bundled up with other goods, or where you may not even be prepared to go straight home but will be forced to leave them in the back of a hot vehicle for some length of time where they will become wilted and damaged.

Choosing a Supplier

It pays to choose your supplier carefully. Every garden centre has a houseplant section, but some are better than others, not just for the care and condition of plants but for choice and variety too. You would expect to see a wide range of foliage species, from the trailing and creeping types to large-leaved specimens and colourful variegated types in a range of sizes and such as a decorative pot, a basket or even a demanding different habitats, from cool, patterned paper surround, to make the plant damp-loving plants like ferns to exotic tropical seem more attractive. Not only will you be ical and subtropical species. Flowering plants getting less of a bargain than you might should be displayed just before their peak not have thought, but supermarkets, DIY stores, towards the end of their natural display, and garages, draughty shelves outside your there should also be a good selection of local greengrocer, or even a market stall, seasonal plants: from pots of spring bulbs to can hardly offer the correct environment for bright chrysanthemums and solanums.

Look out for dull foliage and dropped flower buds when buying hybrid gloxinias; this is a sign that the air is too dry.

Check that the plants are adequately labelled with the full name and favoured conditions of each specimen; some of the more up-to-date garden centres have introduced a computerized fact sheet, issued automatically at the checkout, for each plant.

If you want a specific plant or are keen to start a collection of, for example, ferns, fuchsias or orchids, it is worth going to a specialist grower or nursery. Not only will they have the best possible choice of varieties in good condition, but they will also be able to advise you on the care and conditions required. You can find out how to contact such nurseries through gardening journals and associations or by joining a club relevant to your chosen plant type.

Choosing a Healthy Specimen

Buying from a specialist source should ensure that plants will be in the best possible health, although if you have to receive them by mail this is less certain. Always make sure that there will be someone at home to receive the package and tend to the plants immediately. Buying plants from a garden centre, however, enables you to choose a healthy well-formed specimen. Look for good, lively foliage with no unnatural discoloration or drooping softness about the leaves that implies inadequate feeding or watering or even some kind of infestation. Leaf cover should be evenly distributed along the stem, not clustered towards the top or looking sparse. Beware of leggy, spindly looking plants that have been deprived of light or were not pinched out to produce a good bushy plant. Flowering plants should have plenty of new buds coming, not be a mass of fully open blooms or deadheads. Check that the soil has not shrunk away from the sides of the pot implying poor watering, or that the roots are not tightly packed or protruding out of the bottom of the pot showing that the plant is rootbound. Most importantly, inspect the plant for any sign of disease or pest infestation, remembering to check the undersides of the leaves too.

Unless the plant is in tip-top condition, do not buy it – even if it is the last one of its type or it is offered at a discount. It is not worth it unless you want to play plant doctor to a patient with uncertain chances. Even worse you might take something home that will infest your other plants.

When you have chosen a suitable, healthy specimen, it should be properly wrapped so that it is not exposed to draughts on the way home – an important consideration with tropical and subtropical species – nor be broken and damaged, a problem with larger specimens. Never transport a houseplant in an open vehicle or with part of the plant protruding from the window or sunroof. If you do not have a suitable vehicle for taking a large plant home ask the centre to deliver it.

Home-Grown Stock

Sometimes friends or family will present you with a plant they have propagated from their own stock. This is an excellent and inexpensive way to acquire good quality stock, as the time and trouble taken by a keen amateur will invariably produce top-quality plants. However, on receiving such a gift, check on the appropriate care and maintenance required. Allowing the plant to sicken, or, even worse, die will not only be distressing but embarrassing, too. If you propagate your own plants (*see* Chapter 2) you might even arrange to swap plants with a like-minded houseplant enthusiast.

Schlumbergera bridgesii – *Christmas Cactus.*

2 • PROPAGATION

Houseplants are expensive and, while a small well-chosen selection is fine, you might have a hankering for a jungle-like profusion that is simply beyond your means. Producing your own plants is the answer, either from your existing stock or by begging cuttings from friends and neighbours – you will find most people are happy to let you have a piece from a favourite plant. Of course, you may be keen to grow your own plants not from necessity but from the sheer pleasure of growing something interesting from virtually nothing, and there are those whose windowsills are crammed with offshoots, offcuts and sprouting pips, stones and seeds. Some houseplants can be grown easily from seed and a limited selection of varieties, such as cyclamen, schizanthus, cineraria and calceolaria, is available from the leading seed catalogue companies, sometimes in plantlet form as well as seed. Propagation success will invariably bring you more plants than you need, so do consider swapping plants with a like-minded friend.

You will achieve far better and less frustrating results if you invest in a little equipment when seriously considering houseplant propagation. Seeds and cuttings – the principal means of propagation – prefer constant warmth and humidity which can be supplied by a thermostatically controlled propagator with a plastic lid. This is available as a complete unit or you can improvise if you have one of the unheated types by buying a heating unit. Alternatively, insert three sticks or canes in the plant pot and enclose the whole thing in a large plastic bag to create a warmer, more humid atmosphere for the young plants. This DIY method is best attempted in late spring or summer when the weather is warmer. The important thing is to maintain warmth and humidity at all times. Remember that the rooms in your house might become very cold in winter once the radiators have gone off. This is particularly true of conservatories, which

*Dwarf forms of Prince of Wales' feathers (*Celosia plumosa*) make attractive and unusual plants for summer pots. Here they are complemented by a variegated* Euonymus.

might otherwise be considered ideal for the raising of young tender plants; if unheated at night, move plants to a warmer, more protected environment.

Some of the more exotic or rarer plants cannot be propagated without specialist equipment or professional skills. But, you never know, you may become 'hooked' and make a hobby of it. Be prepared for a

10 · *Practical Indoor Gardening*

Young plants in an electrically heated propagator. A pre-set temperature can be maintained while a properly ventilated plastic lid keeps humidity levels high.

certain percentage of failures even with the plants which are easy to propagate; it may just be that conditions were not quite right or that it was the wrong time of year. Always take more cuttings than you need and do not be discouraged if you need to try again.

Propagating by Division

Plants that form clumps of growth can be propagated simply by dividing the parent plant into smaller pieces and growing each piece into a new plant. *Helxine*, primulas and ferns are examples of plants that can usually be grown from existing segments. The best time to divide plants is in the spring or early summer when conditions are right to allow the divided plants plenty of time in which to grow and repair the damaged tissue. When a plant becomes too large and needs repotting or regenerating is a good time to consider dividing it. Remove

African violets can be propagated by division: once the plant is removed from its pot, you can see three distinct clumps which can be gently teased apart to make new plants.

Propagation · 11

the plant from its pot and examine it carefully for natural segments which can be pulled or cut away to form new plants. Each should include some roots which must be teased gently apart from the main plant and potted separately in a suitable growing medium.

Propagating from Offsets

Some plants like *Hippeastrum* and *Sprekelia* produce offsets or small shoots beside the parent plant which are, in fact, growing off the same rootstock or from tiny bulbils loosely attached to the main bulb. These are easily detached and replanted in separate pots. Try to take as much root as possible with the new shoot. Again, this is best done when the plant is approaching its main growing season so that it has plenty of strength to recover and the new plants have a good chance to establish themselves.

Propagating by Ground Layering

Climbing and trailing species of houseplant, such as *Fittonia* and ivies (*Hedera*), can often be successfully propagated by ground layering, provided you have the patience to wait for the stems to root. All you need to do is pin or peg down a leading shoot into a nearby pot of compost using a piece of wire, a staple or a hairpin. When this has rooted it can be neatly severed from the parent plant. Some people like to put a little nick in the stem where it touches the soil to encourage it to root, but this is not essential.

You will often see an extra shoot growing beside your stately Hippeastrum. This indicates the presence of an offset or bulbil growing alongside the mother bulb in the compost.

12 · *Practical Indoor Gardening*

Trailing plants, such as ivies, can be propagated by ground layering. Simply peg a suitable shoot into another pot of compost then sever it from the parent plant when it has established roots.

Propagating by Air Layering

When older specimens of *Ficus elastica*, *Monstera* and *Philodendron* have become rather large or lost their lower leaves, their thick stems make them suitable for air layering, a reliable if sometimes slow process. Cut into the stem with a sharp knife at a point no more than 30cm (1ft) from the tip of the plant and about 2.5cm (1in) below a healthy leaf joint. Insert a matchstick or piece of plastic into this nick to keep it open and wrap damp sphagnum moss about 2.5cm (1in) above and below the cut. Then cover the whole area with plastic film tied in place with string to keep the moss moist. After a while you will be able to see roots forming underneath the plastic; at this point the stem can be detached and the new plant potted up separately.

Propagating from Stem Cuttings

Any plant that grows by means of stems — this includes a great many of the more popular houseplant species — can be propagated through stem cuttings. Cut off the top of the plant, removing all but the top two or three pairs of leaves, and make a clean cut just below one of the leaf nodes where the leaf stalk joins the stem, to allow the plant's natural hormones to promote root growth. The cutting must then be pushed gently into a sandy compost and placed in a warm, humid environment — preferably a purpose-made propagator — until it is rooted. The best time to take stem cuttings is in late spring or summer, although you can still achieve success with plants such as geraniums in late summer to autumn. Some houseplants, like *Dieffenbachia*, produce a thick cane-like stem and, when these become older and unattractive as the lower leaves are lost, they can be rejuvenated simply by taking the leafy top off the stem to make a new plant as described above.

Helxine Sometimes called mind your own business, *Helxine* grows well in moist compost to create a low mat of tiny round green leaves. It looks particularly good allowed to make a pompom dome above a terracotta pot or encouraged to spread across shallow, dish-like containers. It will flourish in both bright and partially shady conditions and tolerates temperatures down to 7.5°C (45°F). Grow it to complement large specimens but do not put it in the same container as a small plant as it is likely to swamp it.

Propagation · 13

*Stem cuttings of the creeping fig (*Ficus pumila*) will root quite quickly if conditions are warm and moist.*

Regal pelargonium cuttings should root in about ten days. Cuttings are best taken in autumn.

Do not waste the remaining cane however: cut into 6.5cm (2½in) segments, each with at least one or two leaf nodes, which should root if pressed horizontally onto a pot of compost.

Propagating from Plantlets

Some houseplants produce tiny plantlets which are easily detached and grown as new plants. The most popular is probably

Remove the lower leaves of cuttings before inserting in a damp compost.

14 · *Practical Indoor Gardening*

***Chlorophytum comosum* 'Variegatum'** The versatile spider plant does not like to be in full sunlight, but in bright conditions or partial shade it grows prolifically putting on a fine display of sword-shaped, green and white striped leaves and a shower of tiny spider-like plantlets on the end of long stems. This plant looks excellent in a hanging basket, on a plant-stand or high shelf. The plantlets are useful for the easy propagation of new plants. Minimum temperature 7.5°C (45°F).

About 2.5cm (1in) of grit on top of the pot when planting succulents helps to protect the plants from damping off.

the aptly named spider plant (*Chlorophytum*), which sends out small spider-like plants on the end of long stems. Another is the prolific mother of thousands (*Saxifraga sarmentosa*) with its mass of tiny offspring on long runners. The good luck plant (*Bryophyllum daigremontianum*), is another attractive houseplant that reproduces in abundance. Pushed into compost until they have rooted, these new plants can remain conveniently attached to the parent plant until they are established.

Propagating from Seed

Root division, cuttings and plantlets all ensure new plants identical to the parent, but when propagating from seed the results are less certain. The genetic characteristics of both parent plants come into play so the results are less predictable. However, this is part of the fun of propagation and it should certainly not be considered a disappointment if a plant does not turn out quite as you expected. Seeds of the most popular houseplant species are available from the leading seed catalogues; not just the shorter-lived flowering species already mentioned, but also foliage plants such as *Coffea* and *Ficus*. Most of these will require higher temperatures than usual to germinate

Propagation · 15

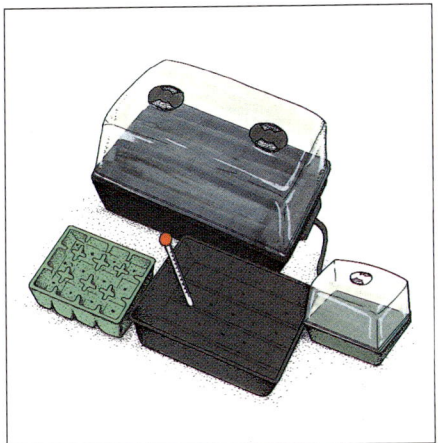

You can extend your propagation activities if you have a heated propagator; even a small one is invaluable for tender plants.

Hypoestes sanguinolenta The unusual polka dot plant must have plenty of light to maintain its curious pink-spotted foliage. Pinching out the growing tip is important to encourage bushy side growth and prevent the plant becoming leggy. This is a plant frequently seen in bottle gardens and terraria, but it will grow in pots elsewhere in the house provided the temperature does not drop below 13°C (55°F).

– somewhere in the region of 21–29°C (70–85°F) depending on type – and germination may take anything up to six weeks. A heated propagator is essential although you could try propagating seed in a heated airing cupboard. A thermometer will show the most suitable position in your home if you do not have access to a heated propagator.

If you love the idea of getting something for free, why not try your hand at growing a few pips and stones? This can be remarkably successful even without the aid of a propagator and can produce some fine-looking houseplants. The pips from citrus fruit – oranges, lemons, tangerines – can be pressed into a pot of compost to produce, ultimately, a most attractive, if not fruiting, light foliaged tree or shrub. A few grape pips might easily grow into a full-scale vine complete with delicious grapes. Growing from pips easily becomes a compulsive hobby and is great fun for the children too. Even an avocado stone can be grown into a fine green-leaved houseplant. Pierce the stone with toothpicks either side and suspend across a glass of water so that the tip of the stone is just slightly submerged. Eventually a good, strong root system will grow and the avocado can be transferred and planted in a pot.

A leaf from an African violet can be inserted in soil to produce a new plant within about five or six weeks.

3 • PLANTS AROUND THE HOME

Unless enclosed in the highly controlled microclimate of a glass container or, on a larger scale, grown in a conservatory, our homes are not ideal environments for plants, however highly we prize them as an interior asset. Humans require quite different living conditions from plants, so it can be difficult to find a compromise between the brightly lit, warm, humid environment they prefer and the cooler, dryer one we find comfortable. Many tender tropical or subtropical species have become popular houseplants, but you only have to see these plants in the wild or in a plant house to realize, as the steamy atmosphere takes your breath away, how different our ideal

The light boundaries of winter sunshine within an average room.

An attractive combination of foliage shapes and colours: grape ivy, maidenhair fern, a variegated ivy and a Begonia rex.

environments are. It is for this reason that it is quite difficult to keep houseplants looking healthy and happy, although a few like the ubiquitous spider plant (*Chlorophytum*) and the hardy *Aspidistra*, a favourite in Victorian parlours, are remarkably unfussy and will withstand a certain amount of neglect. If you choose your plants wisely you will surely give them a better chance of survival.

What usually happens is that you think 'a plant would be nice here on the windowsill' or 'I could do with a trailing something-or-other on this shelf, and a colourful flowering plant would look just right in that corner.' The best approach is to assess the light/warmth potential of that particular position then choose a plant to suit it. This will help to prevent disappointment and a waste of money in a few months when a wrongly placed plant simply gives up and dies.

Warmth and Light

The correct warmth can be surprisingly difficult to achieve. Even if a good constant temperature is maintained in the house during the day, few of us are inclined to

Plants Around The Home · 17

waste money heating all the rooms at night when temperatures can drop quite dramatically. Also, temperatures tend to fluctuate within a room, being relatively chilly away from the radiators and far too hot for plants near them. All plants have a minimum temperature below which they will begin to suffer. This is often indicated on their care label. They can cope with an occasional drop below this provided the soil is relatively dry, but continuously keeping them at the wrong temperature will take its toll. Frost is the real killer for all houseplants. Be wary in winter of closing the curtains and trapping your plants in the sub-zero zone between curtains and window.

Pretty Plectranthus coleoides 'Variegata' *needs a well-lit windowsill to maintain that attractive cream-edged foliage.*

*Grape ivy (*Rhoicissus rhomboidea*) will thrive in partial shade, making it a useful trailing and climbing plant for difficult corners.*

Light levels are even more difficult to assess. Most plants prefer light conditions, but a really sunny windowsill is invariably too bright for all but the desert plants such as cacti. Away from the window the level of light begins to drop surprisingly rapidly – a photographer's light meter will give you some idea of why so many plants fail to flourish towards the middle or back of the room. In winter those light levels are further reduced. Plants' light requirements tend to fall within one of five categories:

1. Preferring full sun – these plants are relatively rare and only the desert species

such as cacti can really take these extreme conditions.
2. 'Some sun' means plants can tolerate direct sunlight for several hours per day.
3. A plant preferring 'bright' conditions does not like direct sunlight but thrives in good light. These plants may have to be moved to a new position in winter when light levels are reduced.
4. Partial shade describes most areas away from the windows towards the centre of the room, which receive some direct light from the windows but no sunshine.
5. The shady areas towards the rear of sunny rooms or in the centre of north-facing rooms are rarely suitable for plants.

Unless you are happy for all your plants to be clustered in or near the window, the

The 'Lime Green' variety of Nicotiana domino makes a very attractive houseplant. It can be easily grown from seed.

Cacti These desert plants will grow in those bright sunny places that other plants cannot tolerate and actually prefer the kind of dry atmosphere found in centrally heated homes. Their strange appearance is not to everyone's taste, but grown as a collection in a special tray or trough they can make a fascinating display – and there are a great many sizes and shapes from which to choose. Given the right conditions some will produce strange exotic flowers – but beware of stuck-on tissue blooms when you buy. The plants prefer to be cold and dry during the winter and it is important not to water during this period.

only solution is to use supplementary lighting. You can buy special light bulbs recommended for plants which can be screwed into spotlight fitments or which even come fitted above plant-holders, stands and hanging baskets designed for indoor use. Alternatively use concealed fluorescent tubes.

Humidity and Plant Health

A need for high humidity is hard to satisfy, as the kind of levels plants enjoy are simply

Plants Around The Home · 19

not comfortable for humans or suitable for our furniture and furnishings. Enclosing the plants in glass (*see* Chapter 5) is not always desirable, but placing plants on trays of damp gravel or packing the space between pot and plant-holder with moist compost can help. Also, planting a group of plants close together will create a useful, more humid microclimate.

A large plate or dish makes a good humidity tray if filled with gravel and water. A combined thermometer/hygrometer is useful for monitoring temperature and humidity levels around your plants.

Too dry an atmosphere has damaged the leaves of this Calathea *'Rosea Picta'.*

Be sensitive to your plants' needs and if you do see one looking a little off colour try to remedy the situation: check whether the soil is too dry or, more likely, too damp – overwatering is the most common cause of death in houseplants. If there is no sign of disease or pest infestation, perhaps the plant would benefit from a holiday. I have used whichever spot in the house offered the best possible conditions for a plant as a kind of 'plant hospital' where, provided I had spotted the signs early enough, a couple of weeks would be enough to put a plant back on its feet. Often plants will enjoy being put outside during the summer if they can be positioned in a spot that is sheltered from extreme sunshine and windy draughts. You may have to bring them inside or at least into the conservatory if the nights remain chilly.

Easy Care Houseplants

Some plants will survive less than perfect

20 · Practical Indoor Gardening

Most gravel trays are hidden once the plants are in position. Here the foliage of Begonia rex *and* Syngonium *almost completely conceals it.*

Aspidistra: called the cast-iron plant, this was a favourite for gloomy Victorian parlours as it survives poor light and cool conditions.
Chlorophytum comosum: 'Variegatum': the spiky spider plant is extremely adaptable provided it is not in direct sunlight. It is ideal for a hanging basket and propagates easily from little plantlets.
Cissus antarctica: the kangaroo vine will survive shade in warm or cool rooms and is excellent for training along pelmets and shelves.
Crassula argentea: the Chinese money tree or jade plant needs very little care but prefers a bright position.
Fatshedera: sometimes called the ivy tree,

Ficus The rubber plant has been a popular houseplant for at least a century. A member of the ornamental fig family, it is tough yet attractive, tolerating a wide range of light conditions from bright to partial shade, and does not require high levels of humidity. Plants last for years with minimum attention and a minimum temperature of 10°C (50°F); the display of large glossy green leaves growing upwards and outwards towards the ceiling.

conditions and a certain amount of neglect as they prefer not to be watered too freely. The species listed here are understandably often seen, but are no less attractive for that, and are ideal if you do not have much time to spare or where your home presents particularly difficult conditions. They can be placed in those awkward positions which are too cool or too shady for most other plants. Being semi-dormant in winter they can survive cooler temperatures provided the room does not drop below freezing. Importantly, they must not be watered at all during this resting period even though the top of the compost may look very dry.

this attractive cross between a fatsia and ivy is surprisingly hardy.
Fatsia japonica: the castor oil plant actually prefers cool conditions and will tolerate light or shade.
Neanthe bella: the pretty feathery parlour palm is another Victorian favourite which does not need very moist conditions.
Rhoicissus rhomboidea: the grape ivy is a useful trailing or climbing plant for gloomy corners.
Sanseveria trifasciata: spiky mother-in-law's tongue will tolerate some shade.
Tolmeia menziesii: the piggyback plant actually prefers cool conditions and will tolerate low light levels.

Living Rooms

Whether it is a light sunny room or cool and shady, you will probably want a few plants to liven up the living room. From a design point of view there are various locations which seem to be an obvious choice for a trailing species, a dramatic foliage plant or a bright if short-lived flowering type.

For the most difficult areas in partial shade you might consider placing on a plant-stand or small occasional table a cast-iron plant (Aspidistra elatior), the pretty European fan palm (Chamaerops humilis), a kentia palm (Howea forsteriana), or the parlour palm (Neanthe bella). All of these will tolerate cool conditions yet put on a fine leafy display. Larger plants that will survive partial shade can be floor-standing in an attractive pot, urn or basket to provide an important and often dramatic focal point. The large-leaved Swiss cheese plant (Monstera deliciosa) can grow a little too large, while an ornamental fig such as the rubber plant (Ficus) can quickly reach the ceiling. However, the attractive castor oil plant (Fatsia japonica) will only grow to around 120cm (4ft).

For sunnier spots a weeping fig (Ficus

*This self-watering container is perfect for an ornamental weeping fig (*Ficus benjamina*) which can absorb moisture as and when it needs it.*

benjamina) is a popular choice, making a small tree of fine fluttering leaves. It does not like draughts, however, or being moved, which will encourage it to lose all its leaves. If you are looking for a large foliage plant you might grow the distinctive umbrella plant (Schefflera actinophylla) which will tolerate bright light or partial shade.

A climbing or trailing plant is often useful in the living room as part of an arrangement in a bowl or trough, or hung from indoor

22 · Practical Indoor Gardening

Ficus benjamina *'Starlight'* has arching stems perfect for a wall-mounted plant-holder or pedestal.

prepared to remove them to a conservatory or special plant house to provide the necessary high light levels and heat once they begin to flag. You should be able to choose a type and colour to suit your interior scheme or, if it is for a special occasion, a table centrepiece to match napkins and cloth. The dining table or small occasional table is an obvious choice of position. However, one or more bloomers can look very effective amongst a group of foliage plants, or a group of flowering plants might be ranged along a windowsill or shelf. Most prefer a bright spot away from direct sunlight. Pinching off deadheads will usually encourage new buds to form and so prolong the flowering season. Also keep a close watch for any pest infestation and treat immediately with a soft soap solution before it takes hold. Chrysanthemums are artificially forced so you can buy them all year round, and they come in a most attractive range of strong, earthy colours. But cyclamen, poinsettia (*Euphorbia pulcherrima*)

hanging baskets, a shelf or pelmet Ivy (*Hedera*) is an obvious choice. Provided the room is not centrally heated and therefore over dry, ivies will tolerate most conditions and are available in a wide range of types, shapes and colours including variegated forms. For a larger-leaved climber, you cannot beat the attractive sweetheart plant (*Philodendron scandens*) which can be trained over shelves or hung from baskets as it prefers partial shade and is fast growing, producing a mass of glossy, heart-shaped leaves. Grape ivy (*Rhoicissus rhomboidea*) is another natural climber that will grow in bright or partially shady conditions: trail it over shelves or place in a wall-mounted plant-holder.

You will want at least one flowering plant in the living room. Most will only be a temporary decoration unless you are

A pink Begonia semperflorens *and a white* Catharanthus *are good companions, both flourishing in bright shade and requiring little or no sunlight.*

Plants Around The Home · 23

Streptocarpus hybrids require regular feeding during the flowering season to maintain healthy foliage and an abundance of blooms.

they die and the soil allowed to dry for a couple of months, the plant should bloom again.

Bedrooms

You want something that does not need much attention in the bedroom as plants there tend to be a little neglected. Light levels tend to be low too. Choose something light and feathery like the kentia palm (*Howea forsteriana*) or a European fan palm (*Chamaerops humilis*) which will not dominate lighter bedroom furnishings and decoration. For a splash of brightness the variegated spider plant (*Chlorophytum comosum* 'Variegatum') makes a good display in a pot or hanging basket.

Kitchens

Kitchens have a warm steamy atmosphere, but cooking produces hot steam and other cooking pollutants so you have to be careful what plant you choose and where you position it. It is pleasant for the cook to have a few cool-looking leafy plants about. Herbs are an obvious choice and an arrangement of popular culinary varieties on the windowsill is practical as well as attractive. Choose from your favourites: rosemary, parsley, sage, thyme, tarragon, chives, chervil – and do not forget a pot of aromatic basil which is too tender to grow in the garden and has a wonderful flavour for tomato and other vegetable dishes. Grow herbs in individual pots or as a collection in a trough and pinch out the tops to encourage a bushy rather than a leggy plant. If the windowsill is a sunny one, you often see geraniums (*Pelargoniums*) brightening up the kitchen; even better is a collection of scented leaf varieties which soon banish cooking smells with their wonderful spicy or fruity fragrance.

and azalea are still winter favourites. Another reliable flowering plant to brighten up the home in winter is the jewel-flowered primula which prefers a cool room. In summer grow bright busy lizzies (*Impatiens*) which can provide a long and abundant display of flowers, or for a bright, sunny windowsill choose *Pelargonium domesticum*.

There are a few attractive flowering plants that have the bonus of striking foliage if you are looking for a permanent display. Bromeliads thrive in bright conditions and come in many different decorative forms. They do not like to be overwatered and should be watered from below as the leaves are fleshy. The calamondin orange (*Citrus mitis*) likes a sunny windowsill where this delicate leafy plant will produce flowers and bright fruit. *Kalanchoe blossfeldiana* is another useful partial shade plant which has attractive fleshy green leaves and the bonus of red, sometimes orange or yellow, flower clusters. If the flower heads are removed as

Bathrooms

The bathroom may seem like an ideal spot for most tender plants as it is light and steamy. In fact, most bathrooms face north and unless they can be heated can be very chilly, especially at night. Another problem is talcum powder which tends to cling to plant foliage, so plants need dusting or wiping down frequently. That said, the hardier types are invaluable for softening the hard lines of all these ceramic tiles and shiny furnishings. Range plants on the windowsill, fasten them to the walls on racks, or hang them from the ceiling in baskets.

Maximum light and warmth are required for these striking zonal geraniums, 'Mrs Henry Cox', to emphasise the strong colour contrasts.

The exotic and colourful zebra plant, (Aphelandra squarrosa) thrives in bright conditions, but not direct sunlight, and moderate humidity. It makes an unusual plant for the bathroom with its strange cone-shaped flower.

The most commonly seen plant in bathrooms is the Boston fern (*Nephrolepsis exalta*), sometimes called the bathroom plant; it produces long feathery fronds that are perfect for hanging baskets or pedestals. *Tradescantia* is another useful bathroom plant which prefers bright conditions; trail it along the windowsill or hang it from bathroom cabinets, the fast-growing stems of colourful striped leaves make a fine curtain effect. The zebra plant (*Aphelandra squarrosa*) makes an exotic display with its fleshy striped leaves and large conical yellow central bloom; spiky *Aloe vera* is also a good plant for bathroom windowsills – it has excellent soothing and healing properties.

4 • EXOTIC PLANTS

Most houseplants are tropical and subtropical species and so tend to be at the very least interesting, if not dramatic or sensational. Some have outstanding foliage, maybe outsized, strangely shaped or impossibly glossy. Others produce fantastic blooms with a brilliance of colour, and weirdness of form resembling something out of a science fiction film. Yet there are still more wonderful groups of plants that require a little extra care but which amply reward the owner with a fantastic display, especially if grown and displayed as a collection of several varieties from within one group. Although modern strains of popular but once elusive plants, like orchids, are far more robust and simpler for the amateur to grow, they do require a little extra effort as their needs are often quite specific and have to be met if the plant is to survive and flourish. Despite the extra work involved, you often find that when you try it you become an enthusiast.

A fabulous Miltonia *orchid: 'Gascoigne' x 'Cindy Kane'.*

*The passion flower (*Passiflora*) is a quick-growing climber with exotic looking blooms. It prefers to be pot-bound and should be kept cool and barely watered through the winter.*

African Violets

African violets (*Saintpaulia ionantha*) are now much easier to grow, with new strains being better suited to the home environment as well as offering a splendid range of colours and types. In the wild on the forest floor they would demand high levels of warmth and humidity, yet shade from strong light. The latest *Saintpaulia* varieties can survive without moisture-laden air and will tolerate some sunshine provided it is

26 · Practical Indoor Gardening

not beating down on them all day. Plenty of light is still required for the plant to flower – although you will find artificial light easily produces the required effect – and a minimum temperature of 17°C (65°F). Most importantly you must water the plant correctly. The thick velvety leaves must remain dry at all times or they will scorch or rot, so it is important to water from below. Also, the plant will survive colder, dryer conditions if the compost remains relatively dry.

African violets, with their striking foliage and exquisite, usually blue, flowers, have become one of the most popular houseplants and there are many societies worldwide which are dedicated to their cultivation. The plants were first discovered in East Africa in 1892 by a German called Baron Walter von Saint-Illaire but did not become universally popular as houseplants until the 1920s. Since then hundreds of top-quality varieties have been introduced: the familiar felt-like, almost heart-shaped foliage ranges from dark to light green, sometimes with deep maroon undersides; and the small but beautiful flowers might be single, double, frilled or crested in pink, red, white and bicolours, as well as every shade of blue.

Cultivation

Although African violets will grow better and flower for longer – sometimes all year – when enclosed in a plant bottle or terrarium (especially one of the miniature *Saintpaulia* varieties), new strains are relatively easy to grow provided they have sufficient warmth and good light. Importantly, they prefer their roots to fill the pot and tend to flower better that way, so do not be too eager to pot-on. New plants are quite easily grown from seed which is available from seed catalogues or, for more unusual varieties, from a specialist nursery. You can obtain these addresses through a *Saintpaulia* society or from a horticultural journal.

Saintpaulia seed is very tiny so it needs to be sown thinly on the surface of the compost, preferably in early winter or late spring. Water lightly with a fine spray rose and leave to germinate in a heated propagator or under a plastic bag for around three to five weeks. A temperature of around 17–21°C (65–70°F) is necessary for germination to take place. The seedlings grow quite slowly but as soon as they are big enough to handle, prick them out into individual pots of compost. African violets are shallow rooted so 10cm (3½–4in) 'half pots' will be ideal, or 6cm (2–2½in) pots for the miniature varieties. Some catalogues offer plantlets ready to grow in individual fibre pots which will get them off to a good start.

Bromeliads Many of this group of succulent plants have spectacular sometimes multicoloured foliage and unusual flowers. They generally prefer bright conditions but not direct sunlight, with a minimum temperature of around 10°C (50°F). The leaves tend to be fleshy and glossy, like this bushy *Guzmania*, and you have to be careful how you water the compact clump of foliage or they are liable to rot. The centre of the clump forms a kind of cup which has to be watered sparingly.

Exotic Plants · 27

Orchids

No plant is as exotic-looking or as beautiful as the orchid. The flowers are almost unreal, perching on slender stems like delicate butterflies or birds about to flutter away. The range of colours and spotted or splotched markings among the waxen blooms are simply superb, and there are over 100,000 species and hybrids from which to choose. The flowers are so spectacular that orchids have the reputation of being fantastically expensive and extremely difficult to grow. This is no longer true, with new, easier methods of propagation available, and with careful choice of variety to suit the home environment. They may cost a little more than other houseplants, but the abundant flowers more than justify this and

Some of the wonderful orchid bloom types and colours available to the enthusiast.

A fabulous display of orchids, mainly Phalaenopsis *and* Miltonia *with a few* Odontoglossum.

give good value for money by lasting up to ten weeks. Some orchids even bloom twice a year and with careful maintenance plants might even live for many years. Although they were initially tropical plants, you do not have to grow them under glass or in a conservatory where high levels of humidity can be maintained — although this does help. There are many orchids that can tolerate conditions in the average home, provided you can approximate a minimum

28 · *Practical Indoor Gardening*

For the keen orchid grower, an orchid case displays specimens to best advantage. An artificial rock face at the rear features crevices for plants.

lighting system. Orchid cases generally comprise a stout hardwood frame as tall as 90cm (3ft) with glass on three sides for viewing the plants and, at the back, a rocky face usually made from fibreglass and incorporating all manner of crannies and crevices for growing mosses and trailing orchids. Alternatively, a tree branch can be artistically arranged within the cabinet. You will probably have to experiment with the levels of humidity, light and warmth inside: the orchids are easy enough simply to keep

A hardy orchid like this attractive Pleione formosana *might be expected to make a good clump of blooms within a couple of years.*

night temperature of between 10–16°C (50–60°F) and during the day between 18–30°C (65–85°F). If you are a complete amateur begin with mature plants rather than seedlings as they are much easier to cultivate and you do not have to wait impatiently before seeing a display of blooms. Do not be afraid to ask advice from your supplier – this is one of the benefits of going to a specialist nursery or orchid grower.

If you do become an orchid enthusiast and would like to expand your interest into a collection of different species, you might like to purchase an orchid display case. This will not only show off your plants to best advantage, but also allows you to control their environment with thermostatically controlled heating, automatic ventilation and humidity, plus (most important of all if the plants are to flower) an integral

alive, but getting them to flower requires quite stringent conditions which may need practice to achieve. Humidity is often (electrically) controlled by a reservoir of stones and water which is positioned above the heat source. Ventilation is frequently provided by adjustable louvres or an electric fan. Temperature, humidity and amount of daylight may be controlled by a timeswitch to create the correct tropical environment in miniature.

Cultivation in the Home

If you are going to grow orchids as exotic houseplants, you must take the time and trouble to satisfy their needs as nearly as possible.

LIGHT
Most orchids will need plenty of light and some direct sunlight to flower: an east or west facing windowsill in summer and a south facing one in winter would be ideal. If you cannot move your plants to a less sunny position in summer, you will need to provide them with shade.

TEMPERATURE
It is best to choose the cooler or intermediate types of orchid for home cultivation. However, do not assume these can survive real winter conditions, especially on a draughty windowsill. Try not to let the temperature drop below their individually recommended minimum, although the occasional drop can be tolerated provided the soil is not too damp. Blasts of heat from a radiator or a fire can be equally detrimental, so avoid any great temperature swings within the room and do not allow conditions to rise above 30°C (85°F). You may be surprised at the temperatures reached on a sunny windowsill so check and shade when necessary.

HUMIDITY
Grouping plants together will help maintain higher than average humidity levels and this effect can be intensified by standing their pots on a tray of gravel or small stones. The secret is to keep the stones permanently wet, but not right to the top or the moisture will wick up into the compost and waterlog it with disastrous results.

Plants, especially flowering varieties, will need feeding during the growing season. However, overfeeding with houseplant food in winter will create a spindly plant. Reduce feeding to once a month with tomato feed.

FEEDING
Feeding your plants can be very helpful during the growing and flowering season. You can add a liquid feed to the watering-can and use for alternate waterings, but only when the plant is active. It is very important not to overfeed so always use no more than half the recommended dilution.

WATERING
Many orchids are naturally epiphytic which means that in the wild they grow not in a soil environment but with their roots draped around the branch of a tree. These would normally be watered by rainfall and, if you are trying to grow any on an old stick or branch, you will have to approximate this effect by using a plant sprayer and avoiding

chlorine-laden tap-water which may mark the leaves or even kill the plant altogether.

The rest of your home-grown orchids will be planted in a special coarse, free-draining orchid compost which must never become waterlogged. Always allow it to dry almost right out before watering, giving a good soaking and allowing any excess to drain right away. If you are in doubt as to whether a plant needs watering or not, it is best to leave it and not take the risk of waterlogging and ultimately losing the plant. You should use rain-water wherever possible or at least leave tap-water to stand a while to allow any chemicals, such as chlorine, to evaporate. Make sure water is always at room temperature to avoid chilling the roots.

PEST CONTROL
Happily, orchids do not attract many bugs, but you can get problems with aphids, whitefly and particularly scale insects. Treat at the earliest sign of infestation: scale insect will have to be removed by wiping with a cloth dipped in methylated spirits.

Types of Orchid

The most popular group of orchids is called *Cymbidium*; these are the blooms you see sold as sprays or as a corsage. *Cymbidium* needs a bright room with some sunshine and a minimum winter temperature of 10°C (50°F). The group falls naturally into two main types: standards which are bigger plants and have relatively long flower spikes, and miniatures which are particularly suitable for growing at home.

Pansy orchids or *Miltonia* are distinguished by their flattened flowers and bright markings which do look very like the garden pansy. This is a useful medium-sized orchid needing a minimum temperature of around 13°C (55°F).

A good orchid for beginners is the *Odontoglossum* which includes many modern hybrids tolerant to varying temperatures.

Striped and mottled leaves are a feature of the lady's slipper orchid (*Paphiopedilum*) which features a distinctive pouch-shaped lower petal. *Paphiopedilum* can tolerate slightly lower light levels which makes it useful for more shady positions within the home. A minimum temperature of 13°C (55°F), however, must be maintained.

Even easier to grow for the complete beginner are some of the new hybrids of *Phalaenopsis* or moth orchid, as they have a compact habit, bloom easily and are tolerant of temperatures down to around 13°C (55°F).

Schefflera actinophylla It is easy to see where the umbrella plant gets its common name: the leaves are carried in wide spread 'hands' of up to ten or twelve leaflets on a long strong stem like a handle. These might be borne in a dense and unruly mass anything up to 1.5–1.8m (5–6ft) high. This plant will tolerate bright light or partial shade and needs a minimum temperature of 7.5°C (50°F).

Exotic Plants · 31

Cacti and Succulents

Modified by nature to survive the harshest conditions, cacti and succulents have an extremely bizarre appearance which many find fascinating, and growing a collection of types can be fun. They are certainly useful for sunny positions with extremely low humidity levels. Maximum light all year round is of vital importance, so plants may have to be moved as the seasons change. If you want your cacti to bloom in the spring you will have to rest them through the winter. This means cooler temperatures – as low as you like provided it is not actually freezing – and a dry compost. Try not to water plants at all during the winter.

Others find this vast group of plants ugly in the extreme but cannot resist the exotic flowers produced by hybrid cacti such as the *Epiphyllum* group or the otherwise undistinguished succulents *Zygocactus truncatus* (the lobster cactus) and *Schlumbergera bridgesii* (the Christmas cactus). Some do not look like plants at all, but resemble a group of pebbles or a spiny pin-cushion and there is a vast range of sizes and shapes from which to choose. Because they are so distinctive, these plants look better arranged in groups rather than being integrated with other houseplants. You can buy special troughs and trays to grow them in which make an interesting and impressive display feature.

*The fleshy jade plant (*Crassula argentea*) needs plenty of sunshine and should not be watered during the winter while it rests.*

Yucca elephantipes This spiky plant loves those sun spots although it will also flourish in bright conditions slightly away from the window. It does prefer plenty of sunshine and requires frequent watering during the summer, yet it will also tolerate temperatures down to 7.5°C (45°F). This plant is easy to grow provided you let it rest, with little or no moisture through the winter. The bright sword-like leaves growing from a thick woody trunk have an exotic look which particularly suits some interiors. The plant can be left outside in the garden during the summer months.

5 • POTS, TERRARIA AND BOTTLES

The right pot or container will display a houseplant to its best advantage. A decorative cachepot inside which you slip your plant within its mundane terracotta or plastic planting pot not only looks more attractive, but also makes the plant look more impressive. It serves a practical purpose too: the outer pot does away with any need for a drip tray and, with a layer of pebbles in the bottom, is good for drainage and humidity. Humidity levels immediately around the plant will also be improved if you pack the space between the smaller pot

Miniature bonsai trees suitable for indoors, like these trained weeping figs, have special containers which are both attractive and practical as they contain the tree roots and keep them stunted.

Placing the plant pot in a larger container or cachepot makes the plant look larger and more important than it really is. Filling the space between the containers with moist fibre increases humidity levels immediately around the plant.

and the larger one with damp compost or coco fibre.

There is a wide range of pots and containers from which to choose. You will probably be looking for something to suit your interior decoration: the container might be plain pottery or highly decorated ceramic, a wooden box or even a basket in a wide range of colours, patterns and finishes. Some are extremely expensive and you will want to reserve these for your very best specimens on prominent display. Others can be acquired quite cheaply or even cost you nothing at all. Look out for suitable containers in the attic or in junk shops: a box, a bowl, a trough or an old basket can be used either as it is or painted,

Pots, Terraria and Bottles · 33

A range of attractive glass bottle containers suitable for miniature gardens. Access through the side makes planting easier.

stained, varnished or decorated to give it a new lease of life.

Plant Bottles

Some plant containers do more than simply enhance the display of the plant. Glass bottles can be used to create a miniature environment for a range of smaller plant varieties. You need a bottle large enough to take at least a couple of small plants, with a wide neck to give you access to the contents (although some of the custom-made containers have side access). The bottle might be clear glass or tinted green. As well as the traditional big-bellied bottle or jar which is available from garden centres in a range of sizes, you could use an old goldfish bowl, fish tank or those large glass sweet-jars with screw tops.

The bottle garden is fun to make and once finished becomes an enjoyable novelty for the home. One of its biggest advantages is not just that you can control the environment within, but that the whole mini garden is transportable. You can move it around the house with the seasons to make the most of the available heat and light; or even move it into a prominent position for special occasions such as dinner parties. Use it to grow those more tender plants or difficult species that need high levels of humidity or suffer from draughts. The bottle need not be sealed at the top as it will still build up its own

34 · *Practical Indoor Gardening*

An excellent combination of variegated foliage forms: Fittonia, Ficus pumila, Dracaena sanderiana *and a small-leaved ivy.*

Miniature plants have been used to create a lush but tiny garden within a glass bottle.

microclimate with relatively high levels of humidity. If it can be stoppered the climate will be completely self-contained: the oxygen and carbon dioxide within will be naturally recycled; water vapour released will condense on the side of the glass and run back down to the compost. Plants flourish in this specialized environment and the only maintenance they will need is to be pruned if they become too large.

Planting up a Bottle

You must prepare the bottle before plan by washing thoroughly, both inside out, dry (using a hair dryer if necessary) cover the base with about 2.5cm (1in pea shingle or gravel for drainage. Next, in a similar layer of small pieces of charc which will keep the compost sweet acting as a filter. You can use barbe charcoal broken up into smaller pie Add a layer of suitable compost – it sho be a reasonably dry mixture – to a dept around 7.5cm (3in), less if the bottl small. A long-handled spoon like the used for ice-cream sundaes is useful for

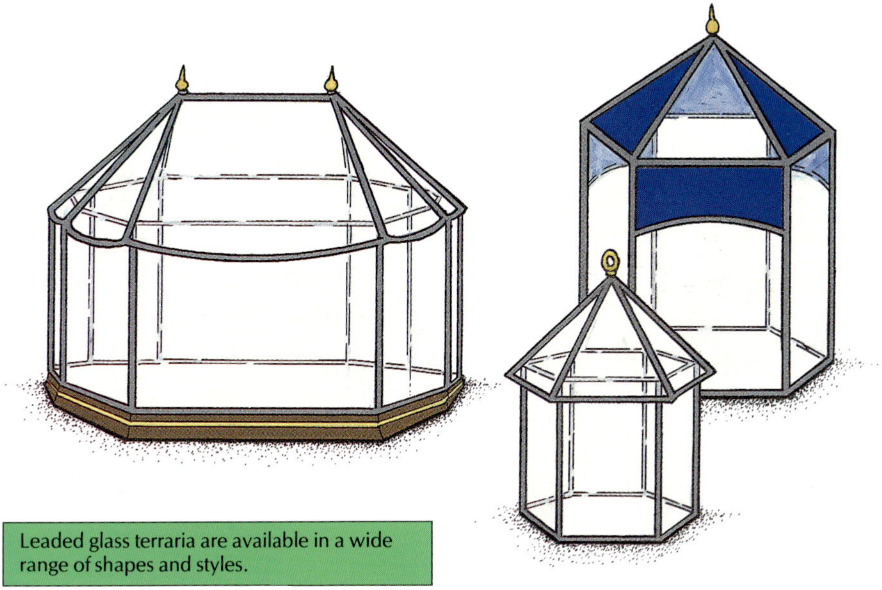

Pots, Terraria and Bottles · 35

Leaded glass terraria are available in a wide range of shapes and styles.

Otherwise a funnel or cardboard tube will do the job equally well.

You are now ready to plant. There is plenty of choice when it comes to interesting and attractive species and it is up to you to choose a good combination of different shapes and colours, especially if you only have room for two or three plants. It is also important that you choose plants with similar warmth and light requirements so that you can position your bottle accordingly. Buy the plants suitably small; they will have to be trimmed, or removed and replaced when they grow too large.

Only use flowering plants if you have easy enough access to be able to deadhead

(left) *Planting up a terrarium: container, compost and plants.*

36 · *Practical Indoor Gardening*

Polyscia balfouriana *is propagated from cane cuttings and looks like a small tree with variegated foliage – ideal for a miniature garden arrangement.*

One of the most popular bottle garden ferns Neanthe bella *with the contrasting foliage of* Begonia rex.

the blooms regularly or these will decay and encourage unwelcome fungal growths. Begonias are one free-flowering plant which are well suited to the humid conditions within a bottle, and which are also worth growing for their attractive foliage.

Try and include a feathery fern specimen, such as maidenhair fern (*Adiantum*), the frondy *Nephrolepsis*, or pretty ribbon fern (*Pteris cretica*). Contrast these with a plant with glossy, fleshy leaves like *Kalanchoe*, the coffee plant (*Coffea*), or the creeping *Tradescantia*; and something with a contrasting colour such as *Piper ornatum* with its pink and silver markings, *Hypoestes sanguinolenta* with spotted pink leaves, *Caladium* which comes in a wide range of

Pots, Terraria and Bottles · 37

stunning colours, or *Iresine herbstii*, the blood leaf, which has bright blood-red foliage.

Plants with tiny or creeping foliage are a useful contrast for even the smallest bottle gardens: miniature *Helxine*, which for all its size can take over if not kept in check; *Fittonia*, a useful creeping plant with a compact habit ideal for bottle gardens; or the bead plant (*Nertera depressa*) which has the bonus of tiny orange berries through autumn and winter.

To position these plants in your bottle you will require a little patience and some dexterity. If the finished arrangement does not look right at the first attempt, keep trying until you are satisfied with the whole effect from every angle. If the neck is too narrow to allow you to put your hands into the bottle you can improvise a few handy tools from household items: a fork and spoon extended by tying barbecue sticks or chopsticks to the handles become a miniature spade or fork; or you can buy sets of tiny implements designed for tending houseplants. You should be able to firm the plants into the compost fairly well. If there is room for more than one specimen in the bottle, try to decide how these will be positioned before you put them in to save switching them about inside the bottle. With only one specimen, a central position is obvious; where there are more than one to arrange

Prayer plant or rabbit tracks (Maranta kerchoveana) has unusually marked leaves and thrives in a warm, humid atmosphere.

Calathea picturata *would not survive outside the warm, humid atmosphere of a terrarium or bottle garden.*

A miniature landscape complete with rocks and ferns in a terrarium owned by the Reaseheath College of Agriculture, UK.

The red herringbone markings on the leaves of Maranta tricolour *remain bright although the leaves gradually darken.*

Pots, Terraria and Bottles · 39

When the bottle garden becomes overcrowded it must be emptied and replanted from scratch.

The inside of the glass can be cleaned with a small sponge mounted on a stick or cane.

and the bottle is only going to be viewed from one position, taller plants should be put to the rear. If the bottle will be seen from all angles put the tallest plant in the centre. When the plants are all in position, you can water them in; take care not to overwater as it will be a long time before the excess evaporates. Add a little water at a time using a hand plant sprayer; you can always add more in a few days if plants look dry, and if there is only a small amount of condensation on the inside of the bottle in the mornings. This condensation inside the bottle should clear during the day; if it does not you have too much moisture inside. Never place your bottle in full sun.

Maintaining a Bottle Garden

Bottle gardens usually require very little maintenance. It is important to remove any dead leaves, flowers or similar debris so that fungus does not have a chance to build up. Plants may also need cutting back if they grow too large. Leaves can be trimmed using a razor blade attached to a long stick and removed with a darning needle similarly mounted. It is rarely necessary to have to water a bottle garden even where the top is open.

Terraria Gardens

Another attractive and indeed even more stylish way to grow a collection of plants under glass is to buy a decorative terrarium or plant case. Their wonderful facility for growing more tender or difficult plants was discovered in 1829 by a London doctor, Nathanial Ward, who found that a fern growing accidentally in a glass specimen case flourished despite the debilitating air pollution of the time. Wardian cases, as they became known, were used extensively by the many plant hunters of that era to transport rare and new species of plant successfully from newly discovered continents. The cases helped them to survive the long sea journey and to continue to flourish in what would otherwise have been an alien environment.

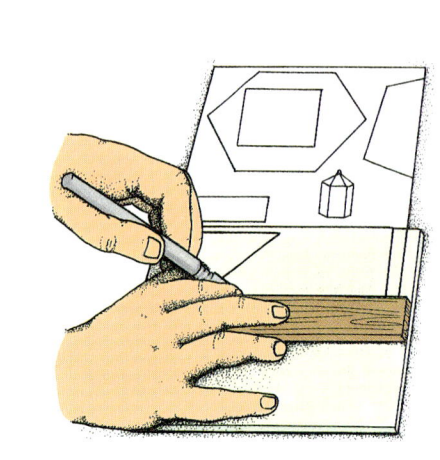

(a) To make your own terrarium, the glass shapes can be cut over a pattern using a wheeled cutter. (b) The edges are then taped with self-adhesive copper strip. (c) The shapes can then be assembled into a classic terrarium structure. (d) Copper strips are used to solder the glass sections together.

Pots, Terraria and Bottles · 41

42 · *Practical Indoor Gardening*

All this goes into one small terrarium: plants, compost, charcoal and gravel.

Today there is a wide range of terraria available in different shapes and designs. You can buy them second-hand in antique shops or new from garden centres, florists and specialist shops. They sometimes come in kit form. Alternatively you might improvise with an old fish aquarium or make your own using glass sections, self-adhesive copper strips and a soldering iron, all available from craft shops. The specially designed terrarium usually has panels of glass framed with metal like a three-dimensional lead-paned window. Some of the panels might be decoratively stained for added interest and the terrarium itself might be any shape from an elegant dome to roofed hexagons or rectangles like miniature conservatory structures. Many have removable roofs, others have hinged doors; all are far more easily accessible than the bottle garden, making planting and maintenance a much simpler task. Some terraria even have lighting built into the roof which makes controlling the environment within even easier. The structure might also include an electric heater operated by a thermostat which offers the option of a completely controlled environment and the chance to position your terrarium in the coolest, darkest room in the house.

Pots, Terraria and Bottles · 43

Planting up a Terrarium

The terrarium must first be thoroughly cleaned and dried in just the same way as a bottle garden. This will make sure no unwelcome growths develop. Cover the base with a 2.5cm (1in) layer of washed gravel or pea shingle, then a similar layer of small pieces of charcoal. You can then add the compost, which looks more interesting if it rises slightly towards the rear; it need only be about 5cm (2in) deep at the front and maybe two or three times that at the back. Because they are larger, terraria offer more scope for plant combinations and arrangements. You can use a few larger plants with your small specimens to create a contrast and a sense of maturity. Plants can be left in

Plants are gently firmed in using miniature tools; these can be improvised using a knife and fork.

An old fish tank fitted with a canopy and integral electric lighting makes a fine terrarium.

44 · Practical Indoor Gardening

have to be illuminated artificially; terraria with integrated plant lighting incorporate specially-designed fluorescent tubes which give out most of their light in blue and red wavelengths essential for photosynthesis. Approximately 15 watts of light output will be allowed per 0.09sq m (1sq ft) of gowing area. Such lights are quite expensive to purchase, but are relatively inexpensive to run and might be expected to last around two years.

If the terrarium does not supply its own

This leaded glass terrarium has an attractive wooden base and a removable roof which allows for easy access to the plants.

their pots and just buried slightly in the compost material, which makes replacing them easier. Sometimes a few well-placed stones, pebbles or a piece of interesting driftwood can be postioned amongst your plants to enhance the landscape, or you might make a real miniature garden with scaled-down bridges, gazebos and statuettes.

Maintaining a Terrarium Garden

The finished terrarium should be sited away from direct sunlight on a shelf, sill or table (strong enough to bear its weight), where its decorative nature can best be appreciated. Larger cases may need a purpose-built stand. If the area is not light enough it will

Caladium The mottled green appearance of the leaves and striking red veining of *Caladium* is a real eye-catcher. Not only are the leaves stunningly marked, they are also large – often growing to over 30cm (12in) long. The plant grows from tubers between spring and autumn then dies back to lie dormant in winter. *Caladium* enjoys a bright position and prefers a temperature of above 16°C (60°F).

Pots, Terraria and Bottles · 45

A delicately planted terrarium with its top removed to reveal the strong purple leaf of Strobilanthes, *feathery asparagus fern and a small-leaved ivy.*

*The pink leaf of the polka dot plant (*Hypoestes*) makes a pleasant contrast to green and cream foliage such as* Ficus pumila *and a variegated ivy.*

lighting and the position is a gloomy one, you can make your own provision by using spotlights. This will not only improve the plants' growing potential but will also highlight the case as a feature. The light source can be fairly subtle, acting more as a top-up for existing natural light. Ordinary bulbs are not really suitable as they do not give out the right kind of light waves for photosynthesis and they produce too much heat. Fluorescent tubes are preferable as they combine high light output with low heat and can be more easily concealed behind shelving, canopies or pelmets.

Once a system for heating and lighting has been worked out, a terrarium needs very little maintenance. Watering will be minimal even where there is no enclosing roof. Simply remove any plant debris regularly through the top or side sliding doors and tidy or remove and replace plants as required. The interior glass may occasionally need cleaning which is best done with a damp sponge.

6 • CARE AND MAINTENANCE

Once you have them potted up and in position and you are familiar with their specific needs, looking after your houseplants can be a relatively easy task. You see them, maybe even touch them, every day which is perfect for keeping a general check on their well-being. It is important that you can spot signs of trouble immediately and deal with them before they become a problem. Routine maintenance also avoids many problems simply by keeping the

The fleshy partridge breast (Aloe variegata) must not be watered during its winter rest period.

A moss pole not only provides support for climbing plants such as this Syngonium, *but also valuable moisture.*

plants and their immediate environment clean and tidy. Adopt the habit of regularly removing dead leaves and other debris likely to harbour pests and disease. If you do spot the early signs of an infestation, you can isolate the plant straight away and deal with it before it spreads. Do not let dust build up on foliage. Large shiny leaves can be cleaned with a sponge and warm water then polished to a shine with vegetable oil, while soft, hairy foliage can be cleaned with a soft brush. By keeping in touch with your plants more or less on a daily basis you will also soon learn when each individual

Care and Maintenance · 47

Large glossy foliage should be dusted and wiped over with vegetable oil or a special leaf-shine preparation.

requires watering, feeding, grooming and repotting rather than doing them all at a set time which can be disastrous for those plants which are not yet ready.

Watering

Watering indoor plants is a danger area: many people seem very unsure about when or how much to water and, under the mistaken impression that if in doubt they should water liberally, have actually killed off the plants they were trying to tend. Sadly, overwatering is the main cause of failure in houseplants. The secret is not to have a set routine but to assess each plant's requirements on a regular basis and water accordingly. It can be difficult to tell at a glance whether the soil has dried out or not. You can buy moisture reading strips which you push into the soil, but more convenient is a moisture meter which produces an accurate reading on a dial. Failing that, pushing your finger into the soil will tell you to what depth it has dried out. In the

this period. Plants in glass bottles and terraria will rarely need watering but when they do it should be done sparingly with a hand sprayer.

Feeding

In the limited environment of a pot or container valuable nutrients become diminished or leached away by watering, and these will need to be replaced by means of added fertilizers, particularly during the growing season. Like watering, too much can be fatal as the fertilizer will become concentrated around the roots. This is a particular danger with liquid fertilizers which can be applied in too strong a solution and too frequently. Pellets or sticks which are pushed into the surface of the soil to release the nutrients slowly are more reliable. Always follow the manufacturer's instructions, but use half the recommended dose every couple of weeks during the growing season only. Never feed plants in the winter.

Light and Warmth

You will have positioned your plants in the home according to their warmth and light requirements; you might even have arranged artificial 'top-up' facilities where a species needs more than natural conditions can supply. Bear in mind, though, that levels drop considerably during the winter months and that plants may need to be moved to a brighter, warmer spot or given a little extra help. Too much can be as bad as too little, so keep a watch in hot weather too. Leaves will become pale and the plant fail to make good growth if it is not getting enough light and also if conditions are too hot. Move the plant and monitor any improvement over a period of a couple of weeks. Keep plants cool during any dormant period.

Hanging plants need careful watering: not only do they dry out more quickly, but some kind of drip-tray or reservoir is essential to avoid spillage. This is Begonia sutherlandii.

summer when plants are growing you will find they need watering more frequently, and you should give the pot a good soaking then allow any excess to drain away to prevent the soil remaining waterlogged. In winter when most plants are resting you must be extra careful as the soil can easily become saturated. Most plants prefer to have the soil almost completely dry during

Care and Maintenance · 49

Spray plants which like a damp atmosphere, such as ferns, at least once a week with a plant mister.

Aftercare

As plants grow they may require additional attention: you may need to reduce a specimen's size by pruning away weak or unwelcome stems or branches that might spoil its shape; or the leading shoot might need pinching out to encourage bushiness. Use a sharp knife or scalpel blade for soft growth and secateurs for woody branches, making the cuts clean to avoid unnecessary damage and possible infection.

Eventually plants will outgrow their pots, maybe even becoming 'rootbound' – the roots filling the container completely and even protruding from the bottom of the pot. Again you will have to step in with remedial action. Plants can be repotted, that is gently eased from their existing pot and replanted in a slightly bigger one (not too big because the roots will not like the change to an outsize container). This is best carried out in the spring or early summer when the plant will have plenty of opportunity to recover.

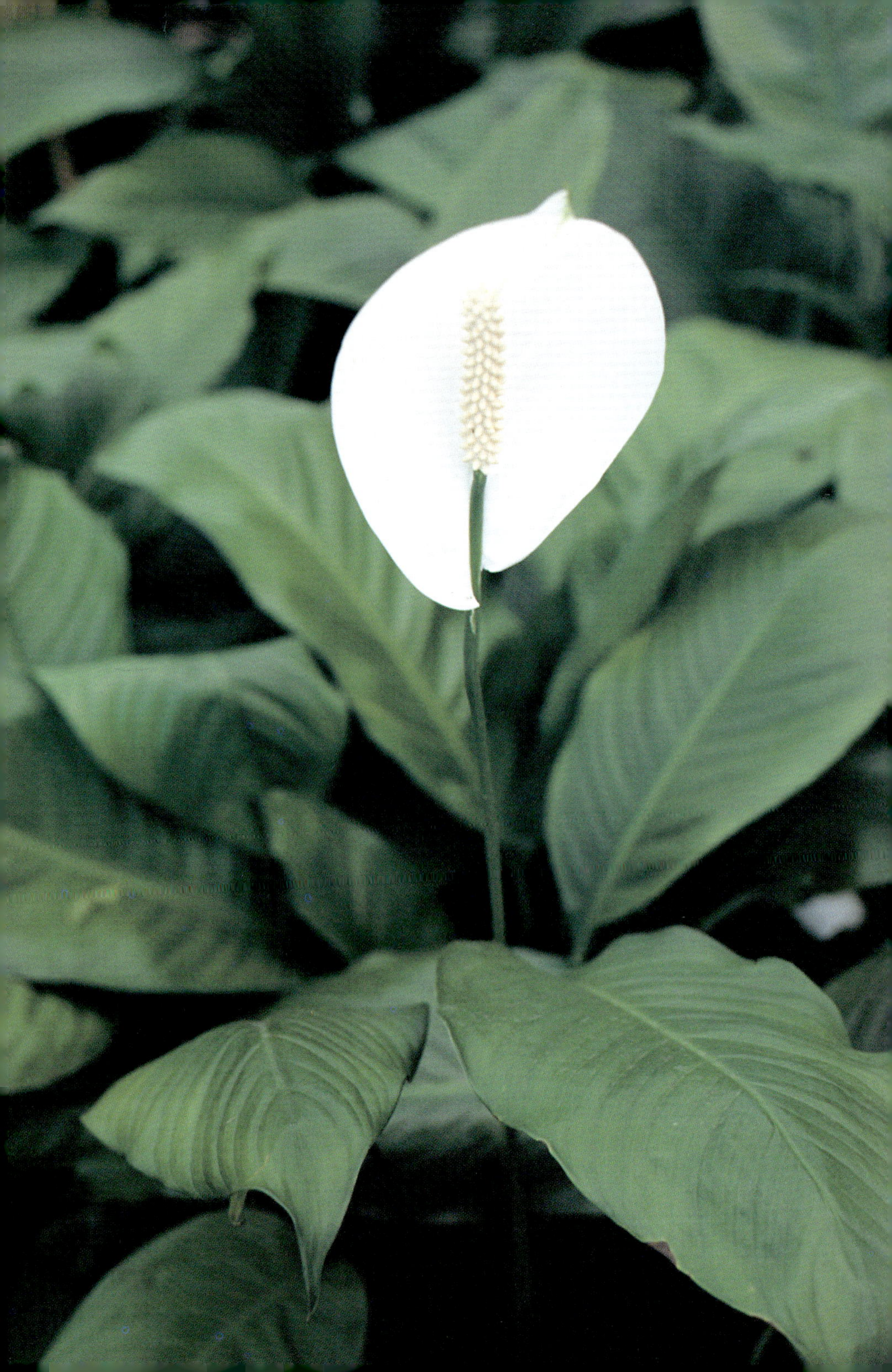

Care and Maintenance · 51

*Very different plants but with similar needs quickly become close companions. Here a parlour palm (*Neanthe bella*) rubs shoulders with a desert privet (*Peperomia magnoliaefolia*) and an asparagus fern (*asparagus plumosus*).*

You should never repot a plant while it is dormant.

If the roots are not too tightly packed and you do not want the plant to grow any bigger, it could always be top dressed instead. This is where the top couple of inches (about 5cm) of soil are removed and replaced with new. This way nutrients are replaced without the plant having a chance to expand.

Plant Health

A strong healthy plant living in near ideal conditions will be better able to withstand any likely attack by insects or disease. Another way you can help your plant is to

(left) *To remain healthy,* Spathyphyllum *requires shade and humidity.*

52 · *Practical Indoor Gardening*

Vigorous pruning will prevent the delightful Abutilon *with its pendulous flowers from becoming too tall and leggy.*

keep constant watch for any signs of infestation and to treat promptly before the condition can spread. This approach also gives you the chance to avoid using harmful chemicals: a few insects can be picked off with finger and thumb before they can multiply. If there are more than a few, try a mild soap solution before resorting to chemical killers. The removal of any dead or discoloured foliage and plant material will reduce the chances of any kind of fungal infection. If your plant is unlucky enough to become infected, it is best to act as promptly as possible with a fungicidal spray.

Fungal Disorders

The two most common fungal disorders to be feared are botrytis and mildew. Botrytis loves damp, crowded conditions so is

*The shrimp plant (*Beloperone guttata*) must be pruned back hard every spring to keep it bushy. Sunshine encourages these strange flower heads.*

Care and Maintenance · 53

A humid enclosure such as this can be useful for 'hospitalizing' ailing plants until they are on the road to recovery.

until the leaves turn yellow and the plant fails to flourish.

There is another fungus which attacks the stem of the plant just below soil level. There is usually nothing you can do but burn the plant and sterilize the pot, but if you feel it is worth saving you could remove all the rotten tissue and nurse the plant back to health by keeping it warm and well ventilated. Do not water the compost unless it becomes imperative.

particularly fond of attacking terraria and bottle gardens. The first signs are a grey mould on leaves and flowers followed by the stems and leaves becoming soft and rotting. Better ventilation and more warmth help combat botrytis. Remove and burn any affected parts of the plant then use a systemic fungicidal spray which kills the fungus on contact and also helps to immunize the plant against future attacks.

Mildew is another fungal condition that can quickly devastate your houseplant collection if left unchecked. Powdery mildew appears as a white powder on the surface of leaves and stems and it spreads quickly from one plant to another. It is important to remove any affected parts promptly for burning and to treat with a proprietary fungicide. The less common downy mildew is more insidious, developing inside the plant and not really becoming apparent

Ficus benjamina The weeping fig is a pretty ornamental fig developed from the humble rubber plant and features a flutter of fresh green foliage on a slender-stemmed tree that, given the right conditions, will grow to the ceiling. The weeping fig will tolerate bright to partial shady conditions but prefers a reasonable amount of daylight and hates draughts which cause the leaves to drop off. Shown here is a most attractive variegated version. Minimum temperature 10°C (50°F).

Pests

ANTS
Ants sometimes accompany an infestation of greenfly because they like the honeydew. Find out their preferred path and put down a little ant powder or gel which will eliminate them.

APHIDS
Aphids are often called greenfly but in fact come in all shades including black, white, red and yellow. They feed *en masse* on the sap of plants, eventually causing them to keel over. You will find them clustered around the tip of the plant or underneath the top leaves, but often the first sign that something is wrong is a sticky residue on the leaves. This is honeydew, a substance produced by the insects which will quickly attract another ugly problem – sooty mould. You can swab away small numbers of aphids and their honeydew with a soapy sponge, but if large numbers of insects have already built up you will have to resort to a suitable insecticide. The biggest problem is that the aphids move rapidly from one plant to another and that they are often brought into the home on new plants on which the eggs have remained dormant in the near perfect conditions of the plant nursery.

MEALY BUGS
You may see fluffy white balls containing a tiny bug on your plants – this is the mealy bug which attacks a wide range of plants. A cotton wool bud or small brush dipped in paraffin will get rid of them provided you can reach all the awkward inaccessible corners they find to hide themselves. There is also a breed of mealy bug which attacks the roots of the plants, especially cacti and succulents. Here the soil will have to be drenched in insecticide or the plant will eventually die.

Distorted shoots and malformed flowers are the likely effect of a heavy infestation of aphids such as this. As usual the bugs are clustered together towards the top of the plant.

RED SPIDER MITE
A scourge of warm, dry conditions, red spider mite can be a real problem among house and conservatory plants. The insects themselves are tiny, but you might see a kind of white web spun between leaves and stem. More likely the first signs you spot will be the leaves becoming mottled and discoloured. Spraying with water sometimes helps to discourage an infestation, but a bad attack will need an appropriate insecticide.

Care and Maintenance · 55

Vine weevils eat away chunks of the plant's foliage.

Check the leaves and stem at the top of the plant for evidence of sap-sucking whitefly. The underside of this chrysanthemum leaf is badly infested.

SCALE INSECTS
Honeydew on the leaves might also be an indication of scale insects, tiny brown bugs which cling to leaves and stems. Wiping them off with methylated or surgical spirit is one of the best remedies.

VINE WEEVILS
These little beetles are hard to spot, particularly as they normally attack plants at night. They attack a wide range of houseplants, not just vines, and are immune to most chemical treatments. The first sign of trouble you might see is the plant starting to wilt, by which time it will be too late.

WHITEFLY
A cloud of tiny white moth-like insects rising from your fuchsia or pelargoniums as you pass indicates an infestation of whitefly. These can be difficult to eradicate as only the adults are killed by the appropriate chemical spray, leaving the eggs to hatch a new batch of pests. You should spray weekly until you are confident all pests have been eradicated.

WORMS
You will sometimes see worms in plant pots – they do no harm and will in fact aerate the soil so are worth leaving undisturbed.

7 • SOMETHING FOR ALL SEASONS

Very few houseplants are truly seasonal apart from a few species such as poinsettia and amaryllis which are traditionally given as gifts at Christmas. Even chrysanthemums are now cultivated all year round offering a wonderful choice of colourful blooms. But you can easily lose any sense of the seasons passing indoors. Keeping your basic collection of foliage and flowering plants in good condition is all very well, but there is an additional pleasure in boosting the display with one or two seasonal specimens for extra colour and impact.

The delicate flowers of primula are one of the pleasures of spring and make pleasant companions to the often bolder, more dramatic blooms of most spring bulbs.

Spring

Early spring offers a wonderful opportunity to display a few bowls or pots of forced spring bulbs in the house, offering the scent, freshness and colour of these lovely plants before they appear in the garden. For forcing you should choose good heavy bulbs with no signs of mould or damage. You will often see them at your local garden centre labelled for forcing, which means they have been specially treated to flower early.

First find some suitable containers: these can be as decorative as you wish – large enamel bowls, decorated chamber pots, bins, baskets – or simply plain terracotta pots. You can buy special containers for growing crocuses which have a series of holes around the sides. You gradually fill these with bulb fibre, poking the crocus bulbs into each hole as you go. A few pieces of charcoal in the bottom of your pots and bowls will help to prevent the soil becoming waterlogged or sour. Half fill your containers with bulb fibre, soil, compost, vermiculite, even old damp newspapers, as bulbs contain all the nourishment they need; the important thing is to keep the growing medium damp at all times but never waterlogged. Stand the bulbs on top of the compost without any of them touching, then pack more growing medium around them until small bulbs are completely covered and the larger ones such as hyacinths and narcissi, have just their necks showing.

When the bulbs have been planted, wrap the whole container in black polythene to prevent the compost drying out and put it in a cool, dark place, such as a cellar or cupboard, for between eight to ten weeks to encourage the roots to grow. Check them occasionally to make sure they have not dried out and when the shoots are around 2.5cm (1in) high, remove the polythene and place the container in a light, cool room (around 10°C/50°F). A little newspaper over the shoots for the first day will help them get used to the light. As they turn green you can move them into a heated room, provided it gets no warmer than 16°C (60°F). Keep the compost or fibre moist to the touch but not saturated.

Bulbs

Crocus can be grown in water provided the bulbs themselves are kept clear: pile washed stones or pebbles in a bowl of filtered or rain-water and position the bulbs between them taking care that only the roots are in contact with the moisture. You do not need to keep the bulbs in the dark.
Daffodils and Narcissi can be grown *en masse* in large floor-standing tubs or urns for a spectacular and unexpected indoor display.
Grape hyacinth are ideal for smaller containers, shallow ceramic planters and decorative bowls. Sprinkle the top of the compost with *Agrostis tenuis* grass seed when removing the containers from the dark to produce an attractive background for the tiny scented *Muscari*.
Hyacinths force well and have a superb scent. Grow them in indoor troughs or window-boxes; or plant in special hyacinth holders which require only water. If grown steadily following the instructions above, they should support themselves well when fully grown and not flop over.
Tulips can be forced if you select the double types: the single varieties for forcing are specially listed as 'single early'. Choose a range of colours to match your interior scheme and plant in bowls or boxes.

Summer

Summer is a good time to propagate new houseplants, either from existing stock (*see* Chapter 2) or from some of the pips and

Tacitus bellus is sometimes known as the Chihuahua plant.

seeds normally discarded with the kitchen rubbish. With a little patience you can achieve some surprising results and gain a range of interesting new houseplants into the bargain.

Orange and lemon pips can be grown into miniature trees with attractive foliage and, if you are lucky, pretty flowers too. Date seeds and grape pips are also good subjects for producing fine-looking foliage plants. Pips and seeds should be planted in a light potting compost and preferably kept at a temperature of around 13°C (55°F) until they have germinated and the seedlings are large enough to be pricked out into individual pots.

The avocado makes a handsome houseplant: soak the large seed in water for 48 hours then suspend, pointed end uppermost, over a jar of water by inserting two cocktail sticks either side of the centre of the seed. The base of the seed should just touch the water, which may need topping up from time to time. When the seed has made good root growth – and you may also see a shoot protruding from the top – pot the avocado up in a container of sandy soil. It is important to pinch out the top growth to encourage a bushy plant.

Children particularly enjoy growing a pineapple plant and it makes an unusual and attractive houseplant once you get it to root, although it may take several attempts to achieve success. Cut off the leafy top of the pineapple, leaving a thin segment of the upper rind. Leave for a few days to dry then pot up in sandy soil and place in a warm position, such as on a shelf above a radiator, to root. Once rooted, transfer the plant to a good rich compost and keep in a warm, light position taking care not to overwater.

Catharanthus If you are looking for a highly attractive flowering plant to grow from seed, check the catalogues for the Madagascan periwinkle (*Catharanthus*, sometimes listed under *Vinca*). The flowers resemble those of the busy lizzie but the foliage is quite stunning: a mass of small, extremely glossy green leaves. The plant enjoys bright conditions and will flower prolifically for a long time if kept away from direct sunlight.

The glorious blooms of Hibiscus *'Tivoli' only last for one day.*

Something for All Seasons · 59

Transferred to a warm greenhouse or a properly heated and humidified conservatory, any of these home-grown plants may also be encouraged to bear fruit once they have matured.

Autumn

As well as planting up your spring bulbs for forcing, autumn is a good time to take a few cuttings and pot up a few roots of your favourite herbs to grow in the house during the colder months. Plant in individual pots and stand together on a tray of pebbles or fill a large indoor trough to make a wonderfully aromatic indoor herb garden. Herbs need good drainage so put plenty of gravel or small stones in the bottom and use a free-draining compost. It is important not to overwater them. Your herbs might also need feeding occasionally with an organic feed if you will be cropping them heavily. A fluorescent tube or special plant light bulbs are a good idea to compensate for shortening days.

Mint grows vigorously and is worth growing indoors for culinary purposes as well as for its subtle fragrance; *Mentha spicata* is the most common mint, but there are many other varieties to experiment with. Marjoram (*Origanum*) is useful for stuffings, stocks and vegetable dishes, and the tiny-leaved pot variety makes a good indoor potted plant that produces attractive heads of flowers. In common with other herbs with creeping roots (such as tarragon), and those that grow from bulbs (such as chives), mint and marjoram can be divided in autumn after the foliage has begun to wither. Dig up the whole plant and tease it gently apart to separate smaller pieces with plenty of root growth. Pot these individually and replace some in the garden for next year.

Strong-flavoured sage makes a useful and highly aromatic houseplant; pinch out the main tip to encourage bushy growth. Spiky rosemary is worth growing for its culinary uses, but its pretty blue flowers make it especially attractive as a houseplant; again, keep pinching out the lead shoot to ensure bushy growth. Tiny-leaved thyme is invaluable in the kitchen, and its miniature leaves and flowers make a pretty windowsill display. These, and similar shrubby herbs, can be grown from softwood cuttings taken in the sumnmer: cut off a vigorous shoot of new growth about 8cm (3in) long; strip off

Stephanotis is an exotic plant which requires constant temperature and humidity to thrive.

> Herbs that grow from bulbs may be divided in autumn. Dig up the plant and, according to the size of the clump, split it into two or more sections by pulling the clump apart with the hands, or by inserting two forks and teasing sections away. Remove the top growth of each section by about a third and plant in individual pots.

the lower leaves and press into the edge of a pot filled with rooting compost. Keep the pot watered and leave in a shady place unil the roots have developed, which will take a few weeks. A plastic bag over the pot can help to prevent moisture loss. As new leaves appear, the plant can be moved to a lighter, warmer position.

Some herbs such as bay and lemon verbena can be propagated from hardwood cuttings in autumn by cutting a woody shoot about 20cm (8in) long with a small heel. This must be pushed into a pot of moist sandy soil and kept in a shady place until the following spring when it can take its place on a sunny kitchen windowsill.

Winter

Winter is traditionally the time when we see azaleas, poinsettias and amaryllis, so often given as presents to bloom once and then be discarded. There is no reason why these plants should not give you pleasure for years: put your azaleas outside in a shady spot for the summer and bring indoors in autumn to overwinter in a cool room. Make sure you use lime-free water. If you want early flowers, the atmosphere must be warm yet dry. The spectacular *Hippeastrum hybrida* (amaryllis) with its impossibly tall stem of trumpet flowers can be encouraged to bloom again: when all the petals have fallen, remove the seed heads and continue watering and, occasionally, feeding until

Something for All Seasons

Monstera deliciosa There is no mistaking the outsize glossy foliage of the Swiss cheese plant. Preferring partial shade, the giant holey leaves are useful for filling dull corners and large featureless areas such as stairwells. If allowed to grow the plant will reach from floor to roof, making it a permanent feature of the home – this may be one plant you will not be able to take with you if you move! Keep the leaves well dusted and, if necessary, polish with vegetable oil and a soft cloth. When it grows larger, the plant needs the support of a moss pole. Minimum temperature 10°C (50°F).

the leaves begin to die back. Maintain dry, frost-free conditions for a few weeks, then move to a warmer position and do not water until you see signs of new growth. Keep the compost slightly moist until the flower bud emerges.

Bright poinsettia (*Euphorbia pulcherrima*) will put on a good display for many weeks if you can keep the temperature to no more than 21°C (70°F). To encourage a similar show the following season, cut back the plants to about 7.5–10cm (3–4in) high and repot in late spring. From the onset of autumn keep the plant in the dark for 14 hours a day until early winter to encourage flowers.

Cyclamen is another winter favourite whose lifespan is tragically cut short by the hot dry conditions of a centrally heated room. If you can keep it in a temperature below 16°C (60°F) it will survive for years, although its blooming potential will diminish.

Winter is an excellent time to create a moss garden. You will need a large flat dish – you can usually pick one up quite cheaply in a junk shop – and a selection of different types of moss offering a good variety of colours and textures. Arrange the different clumps of moss on the dish, making sure none of them overlap the edge or they will wick away all the moisture. Place in a reasonably cool, shady position – definitely not in a dry, centrally heated room – and spray with water about once a week. Add primrose or violet plants to the dish for extra interest.

A Miniature Garden

Alternatively it can be fun to make a miniature indoor garden while the main garden is out of bounds. You can use any kind of container, a meat dish, bowl or baking tin, to provide a focal point on table, cupboard, shelf or sill. Cover the base with a layer of small pebbles for drainage then with a thin layer of leaves, peat or coco-fibre. Add the soil, then the plants and features: dwarf evergreen piceas and tiny conifers as trees, miniature roses, sedums, miniature bulbs – sow grass and cut with scissors to create lawns. Small pieces of stone or slate are useful for building tiny paths and walls.

# GLOSSARY

Acid Soil with little or no lime content.
Aerial root Root which grows from the stem above ground rather than below it.
Air layering Method of propagation (see page 12).
Annual Plant which completes its life cycle within a single year.
Axil Angle at which a leaf or leaf stalk joins a stem and from which a flower bud often grows.

Bedding plant Usually an annual flowering or decorative foliage plant used to create a temporary display in bed, border or container.
Bicolour A flower with petals in two shades.
Biennial A plant which flowers and dies in its second year.
Bract Modified leaf, often colourful, which looks more like a petal.
Break Development of side shoots: this can be artificially induced by removing the growing tip of the plant.
Bulb Swollen underground organ which feeds a plant through its dormant phase.
Bulbil A small offshoot bulb which usually grows from the mother bulb.

Compost Sterilized potting mixture which may or may not contain soil and which contains a balanced mix of nutrients.
Corm Swollen plant stem which, like a bulb, sustains a plant while it is in its dormant phase.
Crown The part of a plant where the roots meet the growing shoots.
Cultivar Variety of plant which has been developed in cultivation rather than occurred naturally in the wild.
Cutting Piece of root, leaf or stem removed and used to propagate a new plant.

Deadhead Removal of dead or dying flower heads.
Deciduous Plant which loses its leaves at the end of the growing season.
Division Propagation process which involves dividing the plant into smaller sections (see page 10).
Dormant Describes a plant that has temporarily stopped growing, usually in winter.
Double Bloom with more than one layer of petals.

Epiphyte Plant which grows not in the soil but suspended from rocks or branches.
Evergreen Plants which retain their foliage throughout the year, shedding dead leaves gradually and continuously.
Exotic Plant grown away from its natural habitat but usually taken to mean an unusual or dramatic looking species.

F_1 Hybrid Plant created by cross-breeding two distinct strains.
Family Major group of plants sharing similar characteristics.
Frond The feathery leaf of a fern or palm.
Fungicide Chemical used to control fungal disease.
Fungus Parasitic form of plant life which includes mushrooms.

Genus Group classification which might include hundreds of species.
Germinate The point when a seed stops being inert and begins to grow.
Growing point The tip of the stem.

Habit Growing characteristics of a plant, such as size, shape and so on.
Half hardy Plant which dies after exposure to low temperatures.
Hardy Plant which can withstand low temperatures although not necessarily extreme frosts.
Herbaceous Plants with soft rather than woody growth.
Honeydew A sweet and sticky substance secreted by some insects.
Hybrid Plant produced by cross breeding different species, genera and cultivars within the same family.
Hydroponics Means of growing plants

Glossary · 63

without soil using a nutrient-rich watering system.
Hygrometer Device for measuring humidity in the air.
Insecticide Chemical used to kill insects.
Leggy Abnormal growth producing long, thin, weak stems with few leaves.
Microclimate The warmth and humidity levels immediately surrounding a plant.
Neutral Soil or compost which is neither acid nor alkaline: a pH of 7.5.
Node Point on a plant stem where a leaf or sideshoot joins.
Offsets Young plantlets growing from the parent plant, which can be removed and grown separately.
Over-potting Repotting a plant into a pot which is too large for its current size and in which it will not grow well.
Perennial Plant which will live for several years.
pH Measurement of acidity or alkalinity in the soil on a scale of 1 to 14. Above 7.5 is alkaline; below 7.5 is acid.
Pinching out Removal of the growing tip on a plant to encourage the development of side shoots.
Pip The seed of some fruits, such as apples and oranges.
Pot-bound A plant whose roots completely fill the pot.
Potting-on Repotting a plant into a larger container to provide more room for growth.
Pricking-out Careful separation and removal of seedlings into another container to give them more space to grow.
Rhizome Underground stem which stores food for the plant's dormant phase like a bulb or corm.
Root ball Clump formed by roots and soil.
Runner Creeping stem which grows on the surface of the soil and which will eventually take root.
Self-coloured Plant with flowers of a single colour.
Shrub Woody multi-stemmed plant that lives for several, sometimes many, years.
Single flower Flower which has only a single layer of petals.
Species Sub-division of plants within a genus.
Spore Wind-borne seed produced by ferns and some other plant types.
Strain Selection of particular plants from a seed-raised variety.
Succulent Fleshy plant capable of withstanding periods of drought.
Sucker Growth produced by an underground shoot or root.
Systemic Pesticides and insecticides which are absorbed directly by the leaves or roots of the plant to set up an immunity.
Tender Plants which cannot tolerate cold conditions and which will only flourish indoors or in warm climates.
Terminal The bud, flower or shoot at the very end of the stem.
Terrestrial Plants which grow in the ground.
Transpiration Natural loss of water via the leaves of a plant.
Tropical Plants which are native to hot, humid climates.
Tuber Underground swollen stem or root which stores food for use during the plant's dormant stage.
Variety Subdivision of a species.

INDEX

abutilon, 52
adiantum, 36
African violets, 10, 15, 25
amaryllis, 60
ants, 54
aphids, 54
aloe variegata, 46
aloe vera, 24
aphelandra squarrosa, 24
asparagus fern, 51
asparagus plumosus, 51
aspidistra, 16, 20, 21
aucuba japonica variegata, 5
avocado, 15, 57–8
azalea, 23
bathrooms, 24
bead plant, 37
bedrooms, 23
begonia Sutherlandii, 48
beloperone guttata, 52
blood leaf, 37
bonsai, 32
Boston fern, 24, 36
bottle gardens, 33–9
bromeliads, 23, 25
*bryophyllum
    daigremontianum*, 14
busy lizzie, 23
cacti, 18, 31
caladium, 36, 44
calamondin orange, 23
calathea picturata, 37
calathea rosea picta, 19
cast-iron plant, 16, 20, 21
celosia plumosa, 9
catharanthus, 58
chaemaerops humilis, 21, 23
Chihuahua plant, 57
Chinese money tree, 20
*chlorophytum comosum
    variegatum*, 14, 16, 20, 23
Christmas cactus, 8, 31
chrysanthemum, 22
cissus antarctica, 20
citrus fruits, 15, 57
citrus mitis, 25
coffea, 14
conservatories, 9
crassula argentea, 20, 31
cyclamen, 22, 61
cymbidium, 30
dead heading, 22
desert privet, 51
dieffenbachia, 12
division, 10

dusting foliage, 47
epiphyllum, 31
euphorbia pulcherrima, 22, 61
European fan palm, 21, 23
fatshedera, 20
fatsia japonica, 21
feeding, 48
ficus, 14, 20, 34
ficus benjamina, 21, 22, 53
ficus elastica, 12
ficus pumila, 13
fittonia, 11, 34, 37
fuchsia, 4
fungal infection, 52
geranium, 23, 24
gloxinia, 7
grape ivy, 17, 21, 22
herbs, 23, 59–60
helxine, 10, 12, 37
hibiscus, 58
hippeastrum hybrida, 11, 60
hypoestes sanguinolenta, 15, 36
home-grown plants, 8
howea forsteriana, 21, 23
humidity, 18
impatiens, 23
ivies, 11, 12, 22
***kalanchoe blossfeldiana*, 23**
kangaroo vine, 20
kentia palm, 21, 23
kitchens, 23
lady's slipper orchid, 30
layering, air, 12
    ground, 11, 12
light, 17, 18–19, 48
living rooms, 21
maidenhair fern, 36
maranta kerchoveana, 37
maranta tricolour, 38
mealy bugs, 54
miltonia, 30
minimum temperatures, 17
monstera deliciosa, 12, 21, 61
moth orchid, 30
neanthe bella, 21, 36, 51
nephrolepsis exalta, 24, 36
nertera depressa, 37
nicotiana domino, 10
***odontoglossum*, 30**
offsets, 11
orchids, 25, 27–30
    cases, 28
***paphiopedilum*, 30**
parlour palm, 21

passiflora, 25
pelargonium, 23, 24
peperonia magnoliaefolia, 51
phalaenopsis, 30
philodendron scandens, 22
piggyback plant, 21
pineapple, 58
piper ornatum, 36
plant health, 19, 51
plantlets, 13
*plectranthus coleioides
    variegatum*, 18
poinsettia, 4, 22, 61
polyscia balfouriana, 36
primula, 56
propagators, 9, 12, 15
pruning, 49
pteris cretica, 36
red spider mite, 54
repotting, 49
rest period, 20
rhoicissus rhomboidea, 17, 21, 22
ribbon fern, 36
***saintpaulia*, 10, 15, 25**
sanseveria trifasciata, 21
saxifraga sarmentosa, 14
scale insect, 54
schefflera actinophylla, 21, 30
schlumbergera bridgesii, 8, 31
seed propagation, 14
self-watering containers, 21
shrimp plant, 52
sprekelia, 11
spring bulbs, 56–7
stem cuttings, 12
stephanotis, 59
streptocarpus, 23
strobilanthes, 45
sweetheart plant, 22
Swiss cheese plant, 12, 21, 61
syngonus, 45
***tacitus bellus*, 57**
terraria, 40, 44, 45
tolmeia menziesii, 21
tradescantia, 24, 36
umbrella plant, 21
vine weevils, 55
Wardian cases, 40
warmth, 16–17, 48
watering, 47
whitefly, 66
worms, 55
***yucca elephantipes*, 31**
***zygocactus truncatus*, 31**